SKILLFUL DATING
for Smart Singles

Proven Method for Finding Love in Today's Dating World

Alex K. Mugume

ACKNOWLEDGEMENTS

I extend am extending my heartfelt appreciation to the thousands of people who generously shared their expertise with me over the past many years. Thank you for sharing your best knowledge and time with me. I will always treasure each one of you.

To all my family members and friends: Thank you for encouraging me to stay in the chair and condense this life-shaping knowledge into the smallest book possible. I could not have written this book without your support. Your constant morale boosting made all the difference. I love you all. You are the best gift in my life. Your friendships mean the world to me. Thank you!

To the Singles: Thank you for picking up this book. I believe that the matchmaking insights explained here will shorten your learning curve, and help you to find the ideal man or woman that finds you ideal too. If you find this book helpful, please tell a friend about Skillful Dating.

I thank God Almighty who makes life and light possible. Thank you immensely for the wisdom and intellect to compile this work.

With much love, enjoy the reading.

Alex K. Mugume

Copyright © 2017-2019 by Alex K Mugume

Smart Spouse Publishers

Chicago, IL, USA

ISBN: 978-0-9742164-9-2

NOTE: All rights reserved. No part of this book may be reproduced by any means without the written permission of the publisher. The intent of the author is only to offer valuable information to help you in your quest for a lasting and successful love relationship. You must make sure that the information here makes sense to you, because the author and publisher do not assume responsibility for your actions.

CONTENTS

CHAPTER 1 *Introduction* 7

CHAPTER 2 *Dating Lessons from Failed Love Relationships* 15

CHAPTER 3 *Dating Lessons from Very Successful Love Relationships /Marriages* 19

CHAPTER 4 *Step 1: Self-Awareness & Knowing What You Truly Want* 27

CHAPTER 5 *Step 2: Designing the Profile of Your Desired Love* 39

CHAPTER 6 *Managing Risks & Uncertainties in today's Dating World* 43

CHAPTER 7 *Step 3: Identifying & Proposing Your 1st Date* 59

CHAPTER 8 *Step 4: What to Do on Your 1st Date* 63

CHAPTER 9 *Step 5: What to Do on Your Follow-Up Dates* 69

CHAPTER 10 *Step 6. How to Talk & Make Decisions on Follow-Up Dates* 75

CHAPTER 11 *Step 7: The Timing Factor* 79

CHAPTER 12 *Step 8. Engagement* 83

CHAPTER 13 *Step 9. Total Commitment* 85

CHAPTER 14 *Step 10. Enjoying Your Love & Counting Your Blessings* 87

About the Author 91

CHAPTER 1
Introduction

Dear Single Friend,

I wrote this book to serve three main purposes:

First, I am happy to introduce to you Skillful Dating, a new decision making skill you will need to succeed in today's dating world. Skillful Dating refers to the mastery or systematic ability to make smart decisions in the early stages of a committed intimate relationship. Here, we are going to focus on the decision-making process, and empower you with the best mindset to make the best dating and matching decisions. I will share the best dating tips and strategies, the best dating advice, and the consequential secrets you need to know to assess your prospect's suitability and compatibility parameters. There are so many important decisions you will have to make, and my goal here is to help you learn how to find your true love from the millions of single men and women out there. Over the next pages, I will share with you how to use this easy systematic thinking method to help you find the right man or woman, who also finds you right for them. It is a very easy skill to learn, and I am sure you will find it very helpful as many others have in navigating today's dating world.

Second, I would like to share with you the incredible wealth of knowledge that I gathered from an in-depth study of over 1,000 adults. These people had an age range of 25 to 65 years old. They shared their broad experiences in building love relationships. Compiled in this book are the lessons and the most important knowledge you will need to know to make quality decisions. Best of all, this study revealed the most useful information you will need to know to unlock the secrets of building a lifetime love relationship.

Third, I wrote this dating book to save you from repeating the same common mistakes that hurt millions of adults worldwide. This is to serve as a learning tool, and a reference book to empower you to make the best decisions. My intention here is to shorten your learning curves and reveal to you the best answers you have always wanted to know in finding your love. This matchmaking knowledge will help you shape your desired love relationship, bring more joy in your love and ultimately brighten the quality of your whole life. Most importantly, make sure you learn how to foresee the future of your love relationship, to enable you to succeed in a big way, and to create more happiness in your life. You will be glad you are learning this decision-making skill now.

How I came about writing this book

I have always loved solving problems, and I was not pleased seeing so many smart single men and women failing to find true love. I was hearing many of them saying that it was hard to find a good man/woman in today's dating world. These stories were so common, and it was evident that many Singles did not have the right pre-dating knowledge to enable them to make the right decisions in finding their ideal lover.

I really wanted to find a solution to this problem that was affecting many people. I was especially disappointed with the high domestic violence and divorce rates. I always wondered why a couple would decide to separate or divorce. At that time, it was hard for me to figure out how two mature people could meet each other, freely choose to fall in love, freely choose to commit to each other forever, and then decide to separate or divorce after a short while. I would always wonder; if that couple truly loved each other, why would they be unkind and unforgiving to the extent of abandoning their mutual dream of loving each other to eternity?

I would always wonder how they turned from being lovers to become fighters and haters and later enter the divorce status, even with innocent children involved! Does it mean that true love last not forever? I would always wonder; nobody forced them to love each other, so why were they breaking their marital commitments? At that time, I thought that those who fell out of love were simply either not serious, or they did not know how to commit their love.

Every breakup story would disturb me, and I started asking friends and everyone who would talk to me at that time. Exactly, how do they do it? How do people get it right in marriage? And guess what? Most of the people told me that a successful relationships/ marriages are all based on LUCK. I asked them: Really, what do you mean by luck? They said marriage is a gamble, a 50/50 chance, you either get it right, or you get it wrong! So I asked what one would have to do to be on the lucky side. They advised that one would have to keep on trying until they got on the lucky side. What? That would mean that one could easily keep breaking their heart or turn into a serial divorcee or divorcer before they get it right.

I kept asking; let us assume you are right: How about the successful and lasting love relationships? What did they do differently to get lucky? They said they were all based on luck; they were based on trial and error. I remember them debating that if there was any formula, it would have been found out already, because there were millions of heart-broken people going through real pain, and these included some of our smartest women and smartest men. Yes! They eventually agreed that they did not know very much about this subject. Many questions came up, but no one could give me the clear answers I was looking for. Precisely, what do you need to do to find and keep a successful love relationship? Not the love that lasts a short while, because anybody can do that, but the joyful love that lasts forever!

Let me tell you a little about my background. I am a risk management expert with a civil engineering background. I manage complex construction projects, and my job is to deliver successfully completed projects within their planned budget and specified time-period. Most times, we have about 30 different trades, all of them coming to work on that site at different times during the construction phase, and this can be very challenging at times. Therefore, I am always foreseeing the project as successfully completed in my mind, and then working it backwards to envision and manage most of the unpleasant unknowns I would never have foreseen, even with the latest risk management computer programs. It is a long-term strategic thinking approach I use to effectively foresee most of the problems years before they were supposed to happen, and solving them before they could show up to mess up our very tight budget and project schedule.

So, all I am doing here is teaching you how to use this foresighting strategy to help you make the best decisions in finding your true love to brighten your quality of love life. My wish is to help many Singles learn this long-term thinking strategy, help them learn how to see the bigger picture at every dating stage, so they can make the best dating decisions without bruising their heart. I believed this would help so many Singles. I was encouraged by many of my friends to share this wisdom in writing, and I went into action right away.

It was a unique challenge, and I had no choice, but to get the facts from a large range of experienced people. Here was my game plan: I had to find out why people failed in their love relationships and why others succeeded. I had to find out all the underlying reasons that cause love relationships/ marriages to fail and ask these people what they would have done differently, had they known what they knew then (at the time of the interviews).

I also had to ask successful people to share with me what they did to create the success they were enjoying in their marriage. It was these background that me to conduct in-depth interviews with over 1,000 adults, ranging between the ages of 25 and 65 years old.

Among these interviewed adults were the successfully married, the unsuccessfully married, the adult Singles, who had quit looking for a lover, those who were still trying to find their mates, and a few who had completely given-up dating to escape the deep pain that hit hard into their soul. My friend, I learned more than I wanted to know about other people's lives and experiences, but in all, this study revealed a very CLEAR ROAD MAP and all the right information that had been missing. It was too much to keep to myself. I was forced to package all this incredible wealth of knowledge into this book you are holding to help any single person, who wants to unlock the secrets in building a lasting and successful love relationship.

Let me tell you some of what I found. Out of more than 1,000 adults interviewed, 280 adults had failed in love relationships/marriage. They had a lot of stories and experiences, and I will only share a few of the testimonies they had in common. Note: <u>The aim of sharing this information here is to educate you to understand how they failed, why they failed, and how you can use their negative experiences to enable you to make smarter dating decisions.</u> Here is what I want you to remember: Learn what the failed relationships did (their shortcuts, their false dating assumptions, their pitfalls) and do not repeat these dating mistakes, please. There is no benefit in learning the hard way with matters of the heart. Then you are going to learn what the successful relationships did and build from that foundation. Thereafter, I will show you this clear step-by-step path that leads to success to Dating; and to a successful and long lasting love relationship.

CHAPTER 2
Dating Lessons from Failed Love Relationships

At the time of tying the knot, each of those 280 adults believed their marriage was going to last forever, but that did not happen! They all learned this great lesson; being good and wanting to be successfully married is not enough on its own, because the success of your marriage truly depends on your husband or your wife! They proved that you cannot sustain a love relationship single handedly; it takes two to succeed. Therefore, it is important that you fall in love with a person who is right for you and finds you right for them; and I will show you how to do this later.

They all rushed to fall in love and failed to see the red flags, which were right in their faces from the time they started dating. They confessed that they were emotionally attached and had hoped they would be able to change their former fiancée(s) habits after committing to them. They learned this hard lesson; you cannot successfully change another person if that person is not willing to change on their own. They also learned that it is not smart to force a mismatch, because it always leads to domestic violence and a future breakup.

They all regretted not knowing what they should have known in time to make the right marital decisions. They were instead consumed by the excitement of the new relationship, the gifts, the new places to visit, and planning their wedding before truly knowing or evaluating the person, they were committing their love to. They learned that, regardless of your feelings, it is vital to control your love emotions and target your dating decisions towards meeting your long-term needs.

They all confessed that it was a costly experience and wished someone had taught them how to guard their hearts from the wrong person. They learned that their hearts were truly the most precious possession they had. However, the other sad discovery was that many of those, whose hearts had been repeatedly bruised, had lost confidence and preferred to stay as players, because they were afraid of trusting or loving anyone again.

They were all pained, not by the divorce itself, but the fact that their divorce was preventable, had they learned how to interpret the advance warning signs, which they all saw during the pre-wedlock period. They learned that making dating decisions unthinkingly and then hoping for the best is being reckless with life. You have to know what you are doing every step of the way.

And you know something? For the many years I have lived, I have come to believe that there is nothing more frustrating on this planet earth than loving or marrying the wrong person. I have come to this conclusion, because, I have seen many people who have lost all their physical possessions and investments, but they soon get over it and do not get bent out of shape, like those who love or marry the wrong person. I think that marrying the wrong person is the leading loss-making venture. I have found that it is easier to correct many monetary and vocation mistakes than it is to correct one single mistake of trusting your heart and life with the wrong person.

I hope and pray that high schools will soon start teaching this life-shaping skill. Simply stated, it is not right to let the younger people out into the dating world without empowering them with this life-changing knowledge and the right tools. It is not right to simply watch our young people repeat the same painful mistakes that we already know about, simply because it is none of our business. I truly believe that increased sharing of this new dating skill will reduce the high divorce rates, domestic violence, and the endless pain that results with a bruised heart. I honestly believe that sharing this skill will empower more people to make smarter decisions that create more families that are joyful, more fun in communities, and ultimately, a better world with happier people and fewer unhappy people. That is why I am requesting you to do yourself a favor and take the initiative of learning this decision-making skill on your own, by whatever means, but learn how to protect your precious heart.

My friend, just like you learned how to drive, and so you do not run through the red lights, or drive the wrong way after seeing the "do not enter" signs on the road, you should not stay ignorant of the basic information you need to help you make smart decisions in building your high-quality love relationship. Please take a break now and digest the lessons you learned here, especially the false assumptions that caused the breakdown. Thereafter, we can move on, and I will share with you the important lessons from those in successful love relationships.

CHAPTER 3
Dating Lessons from Very Successful Love Relationships / Marriages

Out of those interviewed, 440 were married adults, and some of them were in their second marriage. A lot of very useful knowledge was shared. Clearly, there was a huge difference between the couples who had a great marriage and the other married couples. The great marriages had something more special, beyond the wedding rings and living under the same roof. Since my goal was to learn from the best, I decided to spend more time with these successfully married couples to learn how they did it and how they managed to create the marital success they were enjoying. I was back in school, and in summary, these were the most important lessons you have to learn as a single person.

Unlike the ones who failed, these successfully married folks did not make their marital choices, based on trial and error! No! They were confidently in control; they all said that they knew what they were doing right from the initial dating stages. They did not make emotional, quick decisions to get married. They seemed to have mastered this one secret, and that was taking some time to think through their decisions before acting. Their thinking was always in the long-term. They had looked into the future of their marital life, as early as before they started dating. They claimed they knew how to choose and evaluate the things that are important in developing a strong foundation for love to grow. They shared so many techniques on this type of consequential thinking. In addition, how to create the love life you want in your future. Read on, and I will show you step-by-step how they did it.

Another evident distinction I observed was that these successfully married people were incredibly disciplined; they observed a certain set of rules, and that is why they were able to see the bigger picture without being blinded by the outer person or rushing for short-term pleasure. Their thinking style was different. They thought only about being successful Smart Spouses. Their thinking was always long-term and always about the future. But how did they make it happen? And as I tried to dig out the answers, I learned the most powerful secret that determines whether you succeed or fail in the long-term. It was simply this: You have to learn to make decisions from your inner person, as this is the only way you will always make correct decisions. I will elaborate more in the next chapter on self-awareness and take you deeper into studying the underlying source of this wisdom.

These fellows had uncommon power in their family communication, how they listened deeply, how they communicated their love, and how they shared quality time, and this stripped away all the myths I had about love relationships / marriage. These were true role models. Wow! I was happy to learn the truth, but sad at the same time, because I thought that every failed relationship should have learned how to do it right before wasting years doing it the wrong way. I couldn't let them go; I pestered them to teach me how they did it, and I am pleased by this opportunity of sharing the same with you. They shared the top secrets how anybody can use this knowledge to choose their true lover and to make their marriage richer and deeply fulfilling.

They shared many powerful examples, and I will share some of their stories in my seminars during the Q and A session. Many of their stories provided great educational lessons I will share with you here. Many of them were spiritual, even though they said they were not religious! I couldn't explain the difference, but many of them said that there was nothing new. That everything relating to love was spiritual. I remember one of them asking, when the Creator of Love asks, "How can two people walk together if they are not equally matched; what do you match?" You have to know what/how to match or else you will match the things that are of little value in a love relationship. Do you match the outside looks or the inside as well? They showed me that if you only match the outside appearance and ignore matching the inside, then guess what; you are depending on a 50/50 chance, because the value that counts is on the inside. Keep reading, and I'll show you how to match in the next chapters.

They insisted that one's true identity was what is inside them and not their looks, status, or possessions. And they argued that lack of knowledge on what true self-awareness is, was the reason many divorced people <u>were surprised to find that the person they married turned out to be very different from the one they dated</u>. And I will share this with you in a few minutes, when we get into the details of this decision-making skill.

My friend, at that time, I did not know what this study was going to develop into, but I was enjoying this unique learning experience and developing great friendships. Later on, as I put all this information on one piece of paper to analyze it at one glance, <u>I was fascinated by the distinct patterns between the paths taken by the successfully married people and the clear pits in the paths taken by the failed marriages</u>. And on a closer study, these two patterns highlighted the existence of another clear path to a successful marriage. I saw that a person, who knows where these risky pits are, could confidently choose the right lover without making the same common mistakes in choosing their husband/wife. I counted the steps of this new path, and there were 10 critical steps where one had to make smart, conscious decisions before moving on. Wow! I was very excited by this clear new path, because it prompts you into making smart decisions for every stage of the pre-marriage process. It enables you to skillfully process your thoughts in a structured way, to see beyond what is visible with your eyes, to think from the future, and to make informed decisions that stand the test of time.

I shared this new path with many people, and surely everybody was always happy to realize that it is truly easy to predict how the future would unfold if they were matched with any prospect. Wow! <u>This proved that there was no need to rely on blind luck. It proved that love relationships are all predictable. It proved that single people today can actually make marital failure a plague of the past.</u> Wow! This was life-shaping knowledge worth sharing in a book.

This is the critical information that had been missing and causing so much pain in many families and, especially, to the innocent children. I could point to where the challenges were, and why people fail to foresee them, and how marital failure could be prevented. And with all these useful data, it was easy to refine this structured thinking approach into a clear step-by-step ROADMAP as a decision making tool to empower any single person to skillfully make good judgment in choosing their spouses, and this is how the *Skillful Dating Model* (SDM) was born as seen in Figure 1.

You see, most people who failed in marriage believed that choosing a wife or a husband was a one-time emotional decision, where you admired someone's physical appearance and possessions and say, I am marrying this person. No. In today's times, success in marriage does not happen like that. Creating a successful and lasting marriage is truly a decision making process, and you have to know what you are doing every step of the way. It is the summation of all your many smart decisions (both conscious and unconscious) in this 10 step-by-step series, which will enable you to find your true lifetime lover from this large open range of Singles.

This *Skillful Dating Model* reveals the critical steps, which must never be ignored or taken for granted if your desire is to create the fulfilling warmth that would last a lifetime. It prompts you into making the best lifetime decisions for every step in the pre-marriage process. It is a powerful tool, because it enables you to foresee and prevent a mismatch before falling in love or wedlock. This Skillful Dating Model helps to protect your future and, ultimately, enables you to influence and create years of enjoyment in your love life. Many of my students refer to this Skillful Dating Model as the Formula for Dating Success. (Chart in the pages ahead)

All I request from you is to digest the insights of this Skillful Dating Model and appreciate the fact that this simple change in the order of your thoughts will actually empower you to predict and create the relationship or marital success of your desires. Thinking in this systematic way enables you to stay right on track to your desired destiny, and this is indeed the needed decision making tool for today's times. I could not keep this missing information to myself, because learning how to choose your right husband or wife is smarter than being sorry with a broken heart. I did not want you to go on this journey alone, because the more knowledge you possess, the smarter the choices you will make. I wrote this book to support you on your dating journey to success. I only hope and pray that you will emulate this forward thinking mindset to create a brighter future for you and your family, and I am going to demonstrate to you how to do just that.

I want to assure you that if you progressively make the right decisions from step 1 to Step 10, you will not only foresee and skillfully create your desired love life. This is your moment to experience this consequential thinking. Listen to yourself carefully and follow the structured order of this Skillful Dating Model in Figure 1. I developed it to guide you to your best love. Let us now get into the details of this formula for Dating Success, starting with the first step first.

CHAPTER 4
Step 1: Self-Awareness & Knowing What You Truly Want

Your journey to success starts with learning more about yourself. Success here requires you to know your true identity in a futuristic sense in order to know who would be suitable and compatible to you in a committed intimate relationship or marriage. This is very important, because many failed relationships fell out of love after living with the person and discovering that they did not love them! Take a moment to think this through and appreciate the reasons I am emphasizing that you start with yourself and think with the end in mind.

Before we learn anything else, I am requesting you to look inside yourself and honestly answer each of these deep questions. I would recommend you get a notebook and capture this information because it would aid you to develop your vision or blueprint for your future. Listen from deep down in your heart:

1. Who are you as a person? What is your real identity?

2. What are your values? (e.g., principles, standards, morals, ethics, ideals, etc.)

3. What do you value the most in order of priority?

4. What are your greatest gifts and talents? What do you love to do? What excites you about living?

5. What do you find most important in your life?

6. What are your beliefs, and why do you hold those strong beliefs? List your reasons in detail.

7. What gives you inner peace, and why?

8. What are the things that people do not know about you? List them.

9. Why are the above issues unknown to other people?

10. Are there things you do not like about your past? What are those things (such as habits that need to be changed)?

11. Could you identify at least 5 thoughts that lead to those

limiting beliefs?

12. Write 5 new positive thoughts you need to believe now to start reversing the previous negative beliefs.

13. Are you ready to get into a committed relationship? If yes, why do you think so? And if no, what is the challenge, and what do you need to work on?

14. What makes you a great prospect for someone else to desire you as his or her lover?

15. What would you need to do to attract the kind of lover you desire without compromising your inner person?

16. What is your mission in this world? (Your purpose for living: write your mission statement down or else it remains a mere wish. You have one life to live; please give it your best shot).

Fast forward your life from today:

   a) How do you want your identity to read in 5 years?

   b) Fast forward 10 years; how do you want your ID to read?

c) Fast forward 20 years from now; how do you want your ID to read? Put it in measurable steps.

d) Fast forward to 50 years old; how do you want your ID to read?

e) Fast forward to 60 years old; how do you want your ID to read?

f) Fast forward to 70 yrs., 80 yrs. old; how do you want your ID to read?

g) If you died 30 years from today, what would be your legacy?

h) Assume the worst; what would you do if you had only three years to live?

i) Let's make it worse. Assume you had 10 hours to live; what would you do in those 10 hours? Who would you see? What would you tell them?

j) What would you regret not having done in your life?

What did you learn from this exercise? Yes, draw the pictures of your future and your dreamed love relationship or marriage. (Remember, your subconscious mind is storing all these images and desires of your heart). Put in all the details in your dream. What would you have to see in your love life to make it a meaningful love relationship?

Having answered the above questions, I want you to re-examine yourself a bit more closely. Too often, it is easy to look elsewhere and critique others when the real problem is with us; we end up carrying our baggage into the relationship, expecting our spouses to be the solution. Take a moment now, stretch your mind, and detect 5 shortcomings you know in your heart that if you changed them, you would be a better person. List them, yes, any limiting beliefs, and the self-destructive behaviors you know are not good for you (and make an effort to progressively renew yourself to outgrow these unwanted habits. There are so many resources to help you overcome any behavioral challenge you might be facing today).

And by the way, the sad truth I found is that most people, eventually, learn how to do this the right way, but they learn it when they are in their late 60s and 70s, or when it is nearly too late. I am sure you have heard older people say, "Life is full of regrets", but it is not for you. You don't have to wait until you are in your late years to realize that you did not utilize two of the greatest gifts that the Creator gave each one of us, and that is:

Gift #1: The ability to create your vision; to decide on the future you want.

Gift #2: The ability to make that dream come true.

And so, if you are Single and you need a Lover, please say YES to yourself, because there is someone out there who is ideal for you. Now you are going to take a close look at yourself and start deciding where you want to go from here.

For the surprise, do this exercise: Close your eyes and mentally picture in your mind your dreamed love relationship coming true with your true lifetime lover. I would like you to focus on seeing your mental pictures when your desired love relationship is 2 years old; fast-forward your desired love to 5 years; fast forward it to 10 years, 20 years, 30 years, 40 years, 50 years, 60 years from today. Sit back, focus, and review those images of your dreamed destiny, edit them to your utmost satisfaction, and save them as "MY VISION" in a new folder in your memory bank. Please don't just read on. Focus on looking into the future you wish to create.

Open those pictures of your desired destiny, edit and make them exciting, and engrave them as your final vision in your heart. These are the desires of your heart, the blueprints of your dreamed love life, and you are doing it right, because this is a DIVINE LAW for manifesting dreams. You have to SEE IT IN YOUR MIND and BELIEVE IT IN YOUR HEART before you will be able to MANIFEST IT INTO PHYSICAL REALITY. Gradually, I am going to demonstrate to you how you are going to manifest your desired destiny without making the same common relationship mistakes of the past.

The benefits of Step #1 are that it forces you to create your vision, and this is a prerequisite for success. Please don't underestimate the power of this divine exercise. Hosea 4:6 says very clearly, "**Where there is no vision, the people are destroyed.**" You cannot break this law and succeed; you have to visualize your success in advance if you really want to win. Ask any winner; they will tell you that this exercise works like magic; it keeps you focused onto manifesting your dream, giving life your best shot, and all this is easier when your vision is specific and clear.

Remember, all these successful people used this divine visualization technique to create remarkable results they are enjoying now. So now It would assist you to have a clear vision of your desired love life/ destiny, your next step is going to be to design the profile of the husband or wife you want to attract.

Nevertheless, before you go to the next step, I would like you to share with you the 20 examples of the differences between living in the inner person –Vs- Living in the outer self. Please study the chart below and use it to shape your future and quality of life. Where do you want to live, inside or outside? Where are your thoughts coming from, inner self or outer self? Where will you get inner peace? Where will you grow as a person? To help you discover more about you, please take a break and journal all the thoughts that come to you after digesting the wisdom in this chapter.

LIVING IN YOUR INNER SELF	LIVING IN YOUR OUTER SELF
1. You focus on what matters to you.	1. You do what the Joneses are doing.
2. You learn from your past mistakes and embrace the opportunity to shape your life.	2. You are shaped by your past, in denial, and live on made-up assumptions.
3. You look to the future and think long-term.	3. You live in the past and think short-term.
4. You live by faith and with hope. 4b. You believe it first, and then you see it.	4a. You live in fear with helplessness. 4b. You want to see it before you believe it.

5. Your life is flowing and balanced.	5. Your life is a struggle with chaos and uncertainty.
6. You identify life with values and interests, regardless of what the Joneses are doing.	6. You identify life with stuff to resemble the Joneses and impress the other people who do not care most of the time.
7. You find joy in living and are always grateful.	7. You are always dissatisfied, and you find comfort in cheating, alcohol, or drug use, etc.
8. You are excited about life, acting on your dreams, values, and talents to create a brighter destiny.	8. You have no dreams, and you feel you are not good enough. You are always whining about how bad things are and how good the past was.
9. You develop thought of integrity.	9. You develop thoughts of dishonorable ventures like deceit, infidelity, etc.

10. You have true unconditional love for your spouse.	10. Any excuse will make you fall out of love, because your love is conditional.
11. You accept your blunders, forgive yourself, forgive others, and you move on looking to the future.	11. You are in denial, unforgiving, and always looking for someone to criticize in order to feel good.
12. You are satisfied, truthful, and happy with your family.	12. You are unsatisfied, telling lies, in love triangles, and always worried that the truth would be revealed anytime soon.
13. You have a clear and defined purpose in life.	13. You have no clearly defined purpose in your life and will fall for anything the Joneses say.
14. You live within your means. You are strategically growing your net worth towards financial freedom.	14. You live to resemble the Joneses. You buy more than you can afford, regardless of

	your ability to pay off that debt. Your liabilities are increasing.
15. You do what is right, no matter how difficult it may be, or how you feel.	15. You do what is easy, ignoring the consequences.
16. Your attitude manifests abundance; you see the cup as half full and nearly full.	16. Your attitude manifests lack; you see the cup as half empty and nearly empty.
17. You are a loving, confident, and strong person.	17. You are fearful, insecure, jealous, greedy, and out of favor.
18. You are thankful for the love and warmth. You are always connected, demonstrating unconditional acceptance of your spouse and self.	18. You show no gratitude. You are easily irritated, always disconnected, and critical of self and spouse.
19. You live in the inside, craving for the things that last.	19. You live in mistakes, craving for gratification of the things that do not last.

20. Your inner person knows there is a Higher Power that protects, comforts, and makes your life more worthy on a daily basis.	20. You have no faith, always worried about how bad the future is going to be, and busy looking for comfort in the wrong places.

Table 1: Living in Your Inner Self – Vs- Living in Your Outer Self.

CHAPTER 5
Step 2: Designing the Profile of Your Desired Love

I love referring to ancient wisdom, because this is knowledge that has been tested and proven right for thousands of years. The first step to manifesting your dreams clearly says, and I quote, "Write your vision and engrave it so plainly, because it will surely come" (in Habakkuk 2: 2-3). Some people call it a Divine Law, and others call it a Universal Law, but one thing remains true; you cannot beat this law. It has stood the test of time. You will get exactly whatever you write down on paper. It works like magic, because nothing speeds up success like writing your dream down on paper. You make it more specific, and more energy is created when you write your vision than keeping it in your head.

Writing your dream gives you a completely new perspective in creating more clarity of your dream. This is a very powerful technique, and at another session, we shall explore more about this invisible energy. All you have to remember is that the universe is here to serve you, to ensure that you get all your desires as long as you are specific in your wants. Right now is your opportunity to create your future; sit back, and look into your future, and write down the qualities of the ideal man or woman you want, the one with whom you will build a strong and meaningful love relationship.

Remember, your goal is to be specific.

1) Who do you want?

2) Who are you looking for?

3) Design her or his physical looks precisely. Their age range, height, weight, style, facial appearance, posture, spiritual faith, whatever you want; it is your dream, but be specific.

4) Take a mental picture of this person and store this picture in your dream file.

5) What core values do you want her/him to possess?

6) How about their attitude towards life's issues, their behavior?

I'll need you to be very specific about their deep beliefs, because their beliefs will influence their thoughts, their decisions, and the way they act in your love relationship. Keep in mind that their core beliefs will also influence their judgments on what is right or wrong in their mind, on what is acceptable or unacceptable in your love relationship, and you will want to ensure that their beliefs are in harmony with yours.

Whatever you do, specify everything you want in your future, including the hobbies and interests you will share, the major life dreams you want to share with her or him, e.g. if you want to have children together, do business together, etc. Do not overlook anything that makes him or her compatible to you, regarding your needs and expectations of the future, your standards, your quality of life, and your definition of a fulfilling love relationship. Think through all that you want, because you are going to have to live with the consequences of this decision for the rest of your life.

Now you know who you are and the specific profile of the person you want as your ideal lifetime lover, but knowing is not enough. You now have to take some action to find your dreamed lifetime lover. Before you move to step # 3 on your journey in creating lifetime happiness, please stop reading and journal the pictures you saw and the thoughts that came to you as you read this step.

CHAPTER 6
Managing Risks & Uncertainties in today's Dating World

This is a very important topic, and it would be a disservice on my part if I did not empower you to get smarter and take total control of this decision making process. Most importantly, I included this chapter to briefly enlighten you on how to foresee and manage the risks and uncertainties in today's dating world, to teach you how to interpret the consequences of your dating decisions, protect your heart, and ultimately, enable you to succeed in achieving your lifetime dream. This is a big topic, but I hope I can condense it in the next few minutes to increase your awareness on this subject.

You see, just like in business, there is great happiness in a great love relationship /marriage, but there is also great pain if you fall in love with the wrong person. But, unlike in the business world, where you can transfer your losses to the insurance companies, in love relationships, there is no third party to carry your liabilities; in a love relationship or marriage, you have to bear all the painful consequences alone. Instead of getting smarter, many singles have given into fear and argued that they do not have to love anyone if there is risk to bear. Every time I hear this, I am reminded of this Anonymous quote, "A Ship in harbor is Safe. But that is NOT what Ships Are built for." Ask any of our smartest senior citizens. They will tell you that you and I were <u>born with a Spirit of Love; born to love, and to be loved</u>. They will tell you that total joy and fulfillment in life is in loving and being loved in return!

This is why you cannot hide anywhere from love, because love is already in you. Think about it. Staying single has its risks and disadvantages too, because love was not designed to be withheld. The Creator intended love to flow and grow, and it can only grow when it is being shared in a meaningful and fulfilling love relationship. For this reason, we are going to spend our time here learning how to find your ideal lover, who finds you ideal to them, and eliminating the odds of falling in love with the wrong person.

That is why the Creator gave you a sound mind to enable you to think through these kinds of life-shaping decisions, such as this one, to protect your heart from the wrong person. This is very important, because marrying the wrong person poses many risks and painful consequences, and so my goal here is to empower everyone who reads this book to make divorce and domestic violence plagues of the past. Now am going to show you how to foresee and eliminate most of these common risks until you find your ideal man or woman, who also finds you ideal to them.

Imagine, here you are, out in the open range with many singles, how will you see that man or woman you wish to be your true love? Remember, there are two ways of seeing them:

1) You can see them in their outer person, the features that every other person sees, i.e., seeing their body, their smiles, their hairstyles, their academic qualifications, their jobs, their bling bling, the fancy car, their status, their outer beauty, those eye-catching tattoos, and any other impressing things you see on them. This is one way of seeing your date.

2) As a Smart Single, I would like you to take it to a higher level and learn to see their inner side that most people do not see. Inside here, I would like you to begin seeing their values, their deep beliefs, their inner interests, their dreams, their attitude to life, their energy, and their emotional maturity or immaturity relative to your needs. And you know what? This is the area I want you to focus on and factor them in your decision-making, because the quality of

this inner side is their true identity that will matter the most to you over the long-term. Think through this for a while.

Okay, so how will you find one man or one woman out of those millions of singles? It is going to take some serious thinking to make the best decisions. II Timothy 1:7 tells us, "He did not give us the spirit of fear, but of POWER, LOVE and a SOUND MIND." All these 3 interconnected forces within you are supposed to work together for your good in protecting and empowering you. Otherwise, if you just fall in love unthinkingly, you will risk bruising your heart, and then you will have no peace of mind for a long time. Remember always, these three gifts are intertwined for your own good, and you will see this demonstrated step-by-step in the Skillful Dating Model.

The common question I get in my seminars is: Can you really know someone's beliefs and values? Yes, you can, and it has been proven true for thousands of years. I love ancient wisdom, ancient philosophy, especially for the simple way they taught people how to live a good and meaningful life. For instance, **"Out of the abundance of the heart, the mouth speaks"**, (Luke 6:45); so, by HEARING them speak, your higher self can clearly see what is inside them, their values, their interests, their beliefs, their energy, and especially the way they think and their non-verbal communication. Since you know the person you want, you can instantly tell whether they fit the profile of your dreamed husband or wife. (If you are interested in learning more about this telepathic communication, please attend our Skillful Dating Webinars to see these demonstrations)

Another common question is always: Will it help if you know what is inside them? Sure, you need to know the true values and beliefs of the husband or wife you are going to live with, and the Creator of Love guides us in Proverbs 23:7, "**For as he thinks, so is he**", giving us more time-tested proof that by evaluating the words they say and their consistent actions, you can truly tell their identity and match it with your desired spouse's profile. I will elaborate on this in a short while.

True, of course, you have to admire someone before you can be attracted to them to ask for a date. But you should evaluate the qualities of their inner person and test them to ensure that they match with the profile of the husband or wife you want. Remember, you take the whole person; you take both the inner side and their outer side; therefore, you have to make sure that you really want both their outer side and their inner side.

Think about it: Most people who failed in marriage were mainly attracted to their external features and ignored the fact that their external features do not count as much as the quality of their inner features in sustaining a love relationship. I can assure you, in tough times, the outer features do not help you as much as their inner side, i.e., their values, beliefs, faith, attitude, interests, energy, and their emotional maturity. You can foresee their inner side in the initial dating stage, and I will show you how to do this in a short while.

In most situations, the people you meet initially will possess more or less of the ideal prospect than you want. Therefore, you have to prepare in advance, before you go out on a date, and predetermine precisely how you will respond to whatever situation you face. You have to determine which personal behaviors or qualities are acceptable risks or unacceptable risks to you. Nobody cares about your heart more than you; it's your responsibility to filter out any obvious possibility of falling in love with anybody with behaviors, which could pose serious risks to your quality of life in the future.

This is now your moment to shape your future. Picture your dreamed marriage; what can't you tolerate in your marriage? It is very important that you determine your risk tolerance levels before you go on a date. Here is why: Waiting to think about this after the date may be too late to make a smart decision, because experience has shown that emotions will always take control over any person who has no specific risk tolerance levels. You may feel sympathetic and become emotionally attached to them, and all those unacceptable behaviors will look tolerable to you, because your emotions will not allow you to hurt their feelings. You have to decide in advance. Where are you going? The sole purpose of asking you these questions is to increase your awareness and empower you to quickly foresee and skillfully prevent a bad relationship with an impostor who is more likely to pretend, lie, and bruise your heart or take you into empty shell marriage.

Acceptable Risks & Uncertainties

These are the undesirable personal characteristics whose consequences may be supportable / acceptable by you. The definition of acceptable is relative and varies, depending on each person's background, culture, age, education, and society's influence. Each person's parameters are likely to be different, but these are habits that have not yet reached a level to signal a red flag. My goal here is to help you learn to visualize the future consequences of these habits and predetermine your attitude and response plan for every "what-if-habit."

Many of the people interviewed found these as acceptable risks, because they knew they could influence change of behavior. The acceptable risks were:

1) Overspending: They believed this problem could be fixed easily if the debt load was not yet so big. They believed they could create more inspiring dreams, budget together, and work together on improving financial literacy.

2) Digital Addiction: They scheduled time for more value-enhancing activities, like reading, business programs, etc.

3) Sluggishness: Most couples had overcome this by doing things together, like exercising and walking together, getting active together, etc.

4) Feel free to add more acceptable risks to this list as you think of them.

5) Add

6) Add

Unacceptable Risks

Granted, you cannot ascertain the future to 100% certainty, but knowledge of one's past behavior can provide useful data for predicting their future behavior. Many failed relationships saw these red flags signaling them to stop, but they ignored them. They assumed that their love would take care of any problems that would arise later. They had the power to decide, but they did not know how to interpret those signals to make a better decision.

These common habits posed the toughest challenges in a love relationship:

1) falling in love with someone who is a liar and unreliable,

2) falling in love with someone addicted to alcohol or drugs,

3) falling in love with someone with a history of abuse,

4) falling in love with someone immature, with a short temper,

5) falling in love with someone who is low spirited and negative, whining all the time, envious, and looking for someone to blame.

6) falling in love with a control freak, - extremely possessive, manipulative, blackmails, or threatens you,

7) falling in love with someone with excess baggage you are unwilling to carry, such as too much debt from bad habits,

8) falling in love with someone with wrong associates,

9) falling in love with someone blaming you all the time and unnecessarily,

10) Falling in love with someone with plagued with infidelity and lack of commitment to one partner.

11) Falling in love with someone who gets irritated easily,

12) Falling in love with someone with tough STDs or tough genetic diseases that have no cure, sexual dysfunction, and the like.

Note: A person with any of these red flags can love, but they cannot be a great lover over time. Also, here is the tricky part where emotions come into play; regardless of these energy draining qualities, everybody has an inborn spirit of love, and everybody wants to love and to be loved. I am sharing this with you, because most of the people who failed in their relationships saw these red flags, but were distracted by their other nice features, and they developed false hopes that their love would change those habits as justification for driving the wrong way after seeing the "do not enter" sign. Now you have this great advantage of studying how and why they made the wrong decision. My intention here is to help you start thinking consequentially, so you can foresee how the future would unfold if you were in a love relationship with such a prospect. As you will see later, timing is so important; I need you to learn to visualize into your relationship future in the initial period of your dating stage, to interpret and stay, or exit quickly before you are emotionally attached to her/him.

The Smart Exit Strategies in the Skillful Dating Model are risk control measures put in place to enable you to cut your losses sooner, before the price is inflated with pain and unpleasant surprises. Just like buying a home, you do not pay immediately, even if the price is right. No. You invest time and money. You get building specialists to examine everything including plumbing systems, air conditioning systems, the heating system, leakages in the basement, cracks in walls, check for roof leaks, visit the neighborhood to check out the schools, hospitals, shopping, train station, to make sure this house meets your needs and expectations. You check out all these before you hand over the money. Let me ask you; why do you check out all these details? You check out all these, because you know that there is a lot you do not know about this home. You don't want to pay your hard earned money for something of less value. You want to be sure you are getting your money's worth.

Although you've promised the seller that you are going to purchase the home, you can exit anytime if you establish that the home is not worth your taste or price asked. You value your money enough that you are not willing to rely on false assumptions. You have zero risk tolerance, and that is why you base your financial decisions on accurate facts and not opinions. My question to you is: Which is more valuable to you, your money or your heart? If your heart is more valuable than your money, then you should invest more time in learning how to protect your heart.

Forget the old strategy of first cohabiting to see if the relationship can work. Even though this has worked for some people, the majority of the people interviewed said it was a total waste of time, especially for women who desired to have children of their own. This is because some had spent as many as 10 years hoping the relationship would work, all those years missing hundreds of opportunities to meet the ideal man or woman willing to value them and commit to true love. Trust me; you can assess your suitability and compatibility without going into a trial marriage or relying on pre-nups or divorce if things do not work out.

Of course, because of the high divorce rates, lawyers invented a prenup to protect their clients' wealth. If you do not know this. A pre-nup is a legal contract that is drawn up before marriage that specifies how your assets will be split in case your choice of spouse is wrong and you need a divorce. Using a pre-nup is very logical; especially in cases where there are children's properties from the previous marriage or where you have inherited assets you do not want to be affected by a divorce. This is all great if both parties are agreeable, but too many people are misusing this legal document to force mismatches with incompatible partners, using it as a backup plan in case of failure. And in some cases, this pre-nup strategy provided no motivation for the spouses to work on growing their love relationships, because they had an easy and clearly specified escape route as anticipated. In some cases, this pre-nup had become a source of failure.

Considering that true love cannot be bought or forced, it is important that we learn the vital lessons from those who have been there and done this. One wealthy man, who had used a pre-nup two times and still failed, told me this lesson. "However many times you have been burned, you should never act or tell your wife that you are interested in protecting your money more than protecting her/him. Never reveal that she is a trial wife, or else your love will start going downhill." He said his previous wife, who signed the pre-nup, started commercializing her chores with remarks like: "So how much will you pay me for child rearing if I get pregnant with your child?" This was all because the pre-nup (trial agreement) had sent a wrong signal to his wife. He further confessed, "Although money is important, a true spouse will bring you the true love, meaning and fulfillment that no money would ever buy."

In search of a better and easy-to-use solution, I developed this Skillful Dating Model (SDM) to communicate to you the existence of uncertainty that must be minimized with smart decisions in the initial dating stages. This requires you to have self-discipline and self-control to make tough choices, regardless of your emotional attachment. You must protect your heart without feeling guilty. You must think with the end-in-mind view of your desired love relationship, and follow these steps to enable you find your ideal man or woman who finds you ideal to them too. This Skillful Dating Model helps you to eliminate most areas of uncertainty, ensuring that you don't mismatch. In circumstances where you are not sure of your choice, you should cut your losses immediately and go back into the open range. You are a Smart Single; so you always have to think with the end in mind.

You must always play the long game - always thinking consequentially. The successful couples advised that you protect your heart by falling in love with a person who is romantically and sexually compatible to you. If you find your true love, he or she will take care of the wealth and make it multiply faster. Therefore, your duty here is to take personal responsibility, do the necessary work, by learning how to assess who is suitable and compatible to you before falling in love. To many of you, it will be a one-life decision. Therefore, your goal should be to make a smart choice, make sure they find you ideal to them. Never and ever attempt to force a mismatch under the cover of a pre-nup or divorce strategy; it is a losers' strategy.

Here is what you are going to do. At every stage during this dating cycle, you are going to choose certainty and eliminate as much uncertainty as you can, when you still can. It is all about developing a zero tolerance strategy for excess baggage you are not willing to carry into your future. Your goal is to eliminate the unacceptable habits that could jeopardize the success of your love life and future. Now you are aware, and your job is to find your ideal lover, who also finds you ideal, and then use this self-awareness as strength to build a rock solid foundation for your love relationship. Take some time to digest what you learned in this chapter, and then we can move on to the next stage of this dating process protocol.

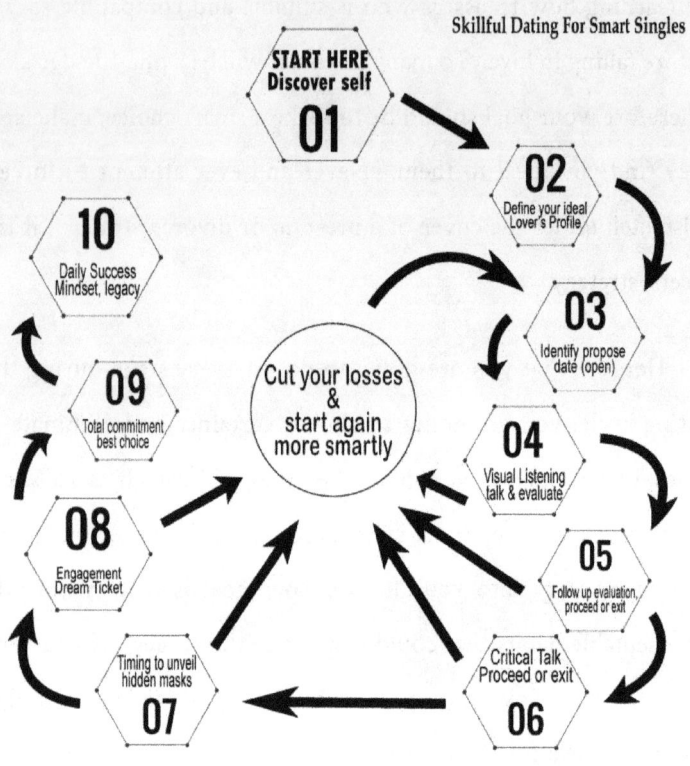

Figure 1.
The Skillful Dating Model (SDM)

ⓒ Alex Mugume

CHAPTER 7
Step 3: Identifying & Proposing Your 1st Date

Now you are doing it the smart way; you are ahead of the game. You know where you are going and who you are looking for. You know the kind of future you want and the husband or wife you want to be married to, and all this is clearly written down on paper. If you are a believer, you should invest in the power of prayer, and ask the Creator of Love to guide you and make your plans agreeable with His will, as advised in Proverbs 16:3.

Okay, you know the person you want, but where will you begin your search? It is easy; you don't have to fly far to search. Begin with the nearest public activities and events that match their values and interests: the theaters, community events, trade shows, parties, business conventions, sports events, in your network links, etc. The fact that you know who you are looking for will make it easy to spot them, as long as they have your desired physical features and are not married.

Your first assignment will be to overcome the fear of rejection and approach him or her in a relaxed and friendly manner, chitchat a little, and then ask for a date to get to know each other. Of course, before you do this, you will have worked on yourself to be lovable enough to attract a date and flow from the inside. You will also have to develop your conversation skills to engage any prospect in small talk, while evaluating their attitude and character in comparison with your dreamed profile.

And here is where your deep understanding of this decision-making skill will make all the difference, as you'll see, you'll now be able to make quality decisions faster and with more confidence. Once you know your dream so well (I mean exactly the person you are looking for), your inner person will immediately give you the feedback whether the person you have met is suitable as a prospective partner in a committed intimate relationship.

Please learn this: If she/he is not suitable and compatible to the profile of your desired lover, please do not hang around them for long. Here is why: Every person has a good side, and you are likely to discover and be attracted to their other outer things, which were not on your priority list. At this stage, please keep your eyes focused on your dreamed profile, create a reason to hurry to some place, and politely move away before you are diverted from your dream. If they are within your desired range, then propose a date and venue to meet again.

The good news is that if she/he is not the one you are looking for, you can stay in this open range; there are millions of singles, and there is an ideal one for you, one who will also find you very ideal for them. The benefits of this step are that you are not just seated, wishing and not doing anything; you are making an effort to make your dream a reality, and this pleases the Universe to work in your favor. Remember the Law of Attraction? The Ideal man or woman you are looking for is also looking for you! So keep the faith, ask for the date and make your dream come true. Asking for the date will create more enthusiasm in you to take the next progressive step. Just keep your mind on what you want.

CHAPTER 8
Step 4: What to Do on Your 1st Date

The purpose of your first date is to get more details about each other. It is not to cut corners to go to bed with them. Neither is it to start talking about your engagement or wedding plans. Your goal here is to screen them and assess their suitability as a prospective partner in a more committed intimate relationship. There are lots of dating cultures; you can visit your nearest library to learn more on dating different cultures. My goal in this book is to focus on the structured systematic order of thinking that enables you to make your best choice.

This is what you need to do on your first date. Of course, you have to look good, smell good, but be yourself, and arrive at the agreed venue on time. Never be late for a date; if delayed, please call her/him in advance. Again, be cheerful, friendly, and relaxed to make them relax too. Start an open and interesting conversation to make your date comfortable in order to give you the important information you need for your instant evaluation. The purpose of this open-ended conversation is to visually listen for their character, ambition, belief commitment, personality, intelligence, authenticity and full disclosure, and emotional connection!

In 10 to 30 minutes, you can get most of the information you need to understand your prospect's character and history. In addition, using your risk tolerance levels, you should be able to make a decision whether to see them again or cut your losses here.

Make sure the conversation revolves around you two and reveals each other's background and character. Look him or her in the eye, read their face, assess whether their words are honest and from their inner person. Great opportunity here! Examine the bigger picture, their personality and attitude. Ask the questions you are looking for. If she or he dodges the question, ask again, and scrutinize the cause of concealment. Listen to your inner voice. If there is no harmony between the vision in your subconscious mind and conscious mind, and you are displeased, because you see no chemistry between you two, please don't waste more time; cut your losses here and go back to the open range of Singles.

If you are pleased, then develop more friendliness, and confirm the next date to get to know more details about each other. If you want, make yourself a checklist to prompt you of all the items you should not forget to evaluate. It is a one-time opportunity. All the time, while they are speaking, read their face and assess whether their words are honest and from the inner person. (Re-read Table 1). Don't start guessing in case you did not understand what they said. Ask the questions that enable you to see the bigger picture, yes, and the bigger picture of how your relationship with this prospect could unfold if you were to live together. Simulate and compare your needs and expectations of the future versus theirs. What do you see?

Using your already predetermined risk tolerance levels, you should be able to tell whether she/he is suitable and compatible to you as a prospective partner in a committed intimate relationship. You should be able to assess all these within the first few minutes of your discussion. If they are within your acceptable range, then you can relax, talk more, and propose the next date to follow-up your dream. If they are not ideal for you, don't feel bad, as if you have wasted your time. Instead, you should consider it fun, cut your losses here, and run back into the open range to search for a better prospect. At this stage, you should focus on your dream and not be guilty for what that prospect is feeling.

At this filtering stage, it is okay to be selfish; you are looking for the right mate and not the first person you meet if they do not meet your standards.

One other thing I request you to be cautious of during your talk is to secretly guard your treasured dream. Your treasured dream is the profile of your dreamed husband or wife; please, keep your dream to yourself! Most players will always ask you for the qualities of the husband or wife you are looking for. Make no mistake, if you tell them your dreamed profile, and they are interested in you, they will pretend to possess the qualities you are looking for in them, and you will be excited to fall in love with the wrong person. So do not sabotage yourself at this filtering stage. Just keep talking; you will know who is who, as we shall see later.

The main benefit of this step is that it enables you to clearly look into the future and avoid wasting time with a heart bruiser, the person who is going to mess your future with less than you are entitled to. Keep the faith in your dream, filtering the undesired prospects out and, ultimately, leading you to your true love.

But, before we go to the next step, I would like to sensitize you on one more important ingredient for success. It is called patience and self-discipline. I mean having enough understanding to deny your flesh's desire for instant sexual gratification. If your goal is to create a brighter future for yourself and your family, then you should focus all your energies on doing it right the first time. However gorgeous they may look, you must avoid the temptation to start petting, because once you arouse your sexual desires, your emotions will take control, and your priority will now become a one-night stand, instead of looking for your dreamed husband or wife.

Don't learn it the hard way. The need for instant sexual pleasure always results in a rush to fall in love, and believe it or not, physical intimacy is a deep commitment on its own. It is a non-verbal voice that says: You have accepted them, you like them, and you have approved them, and with this inner bond, your love emotions will very likely turn color blind to the red flags. Don't go there yet! Your dream of a rich love relationship as your destiny would be stolen, simply because you lacked patience and self-control. That is why you should do the critical evaluation first. After all, you are going to have them forever, so what is the rush about?

As a Smart Single, you should avoid or minimize your alcohol intake on this day. Experience has shown that decisions made under the influence of alcohol or similar substances are only good for the short-term. These substances will usually impair your judgment and make you color blind. The red flag will look green in color, and before you know it, these substances will get you married to the wrong person for the wrong reasons. If you can, please keep sober when you are thinking through this very important and life-shaping decision. If you are satisfied with your initial evaluation, you can now move on to the next step and continue this process of making your greatest decisions.

CHAPTER 9
Step 5: What to Do on Your Follow-Up Dates

The purpose of this stage is to ensure that he or she possesses the characteristics you want. As a Smart Single, your responsibility here is to eliminate the baggage that is always hidden in the details. I would like you to begin evaluating whether you can both be committed to a lasting love relationship.

1) Can you really have an intimate and fulfilling warm relationship with this person?

2) Can he or she treasure your love?

3) Can you really trust her/him to make a great and lasting love relationship?

What you are doing here is to clarify the vision of your love relationship.

I talked about risks earlier, and I know this is one. You are going to make yourself exposed to rejection, and you must accept this as a smart approach. You will have to open up and talk about yourself during your conversation with your prospect on this follow up date. It is only fair that you should take the lead and open up first before they open up to you. And while they are talking to you, I need you to start evaluating their choice of words, their beliefs, their strong and weak personal characteristics, and match your similarities and differences in respect to your desired destiny you are trying to create. What pictures do you see? Remember, it is all predictable. You can foretell how the future is going to unfold by evaluating all these factors.

As a Smart Single, please do not ignore anything that you think will matter to you in your future. Get the courage. I know the devil is always in the details, but do not be shy. This is the best time to ask the right questions that will help you to understand their growing up, their deep beliefs, their core values, their previous marriages if any, their hobbies, their careers, and especially, where they are going and the future they envision. Please, do not be tricked with vague words. Do not start guessing what they meant for fear of rejection. Ask all the details you need for your evaluation and make sure they open up to you; otherwise, what other proof do you need to reveal to you that they will not open up in your love relationship or marriage, if they do not open up now?

Again, as you evaluate them, you also have a duty to inform them about the real you to enable them to evaluate you. Too often, it is easy to demand of others and not do the same thing. You should reveal all there is about you and your past to help them make a better informed decision in deciding whether you fit their desired profile. I know it is uncomfortable, but you have to tell them all about your past, your habits, your previous marriages and children, if any, your genetic problems, your allergies, and whatever challenges you think they should know! Rather than wait for them to find out and reject you later when you are deep in your love relationship, you would rather stay in the open range, because your true lifetime lover will accept you as you are.

As you listen to all their responses, evaluate their inner person in relation to your dreamed profile of your desired husband or wife; do they fit your dream? Remember ancient wisdom teaches us, "**As you think so are you**" (Proverbs 23:7), and poses this question, "**How can two walk together if they are not equally matched?**" (Amos 3:3). There is a lot of power in these two ancient quotes, but I want you to focus on the wisdom that hits the spot on what you should match in building a lasting love relationships.

As a Skillful Dater, interested in developing a high-quality love life, you should focus on matching your style of thinking, your values, your beliefs, your interests, your dreams, and all the things that make each of you happy about living. You should also match your needs and expectations from the love relationship. These are so many features to match and so many decisions to make. Keep in mind that you are going to inherit the whole package, both their outer and inner person; therefore, you have to make sure that your choice is a winning decision that will last the test of time.

In fact, the successfully married folks summarized it this way; every similarity in your core values, your deep beliefs, your interests, your faith, and your dreams will be a powerful force that will guarantee a lifetime of joy in your whole family. Get this revelation too, the reverse is also true! Every major difference in these inner personal qualities would without a doubt hurt you, because you will always be disagreeing on the things you value the most in your life. Spend a minute, think about this piece of wisdom, and use it as a benchmark in all your next many decisions you would make.

Here, you want to make sure that you are investing your love and destiny in the hands of the person who is right for you and as well finds you right for them, while eliminating any possibility of a mismatch. Remember these basic questions before you make your final decision to fall in love with them.

1) Do you think nearly the same, regarding your needs and expectations from your love relationship?

2) If yes, fantastic! If not, where is the contradiction? Examine it.

3) What could be the consequences from a futuristic point of view?

Get all the facts in order; ask for any clarification on any incompatible story that sounds like a red flag, regardless of whether it makes him or her uncomfortable. You will be glad you did.

The benefits of this Step are that it helps you to clarify whether he or she has the potential to make a great lover /wife or husband. This step gets you closer to your ideal lifetime lover and enables you to create your dreamed marital destiny. At any of these stages, if you are not happy with them, it is easier to cut your losses now, because you are not yet emotionally attached to them. However, if your conscious mind is in harmony with the vision in your subconscious mind, and you are satisfied with your selection, please proceed to the next step.

CHAPTER 10
Step6. How to Talk & Make Decisions on Follow-Up Dates

The purpose of this step is to clarify your inner understanding of each other's long-term needs and expectations from your committed intimate relationship. Here, your goal is to confirm that you are making a smarter decision and not compromising your lifetime dream with false assumptions. You are doing all you can to ensure total disclosure about their past in order to make better decisions. In this step, you are using all the information available to you. Please pay attention to their past and present attitudes and behaviors.

I know there is no guarantee of their future behavior, but what you see today is the best indicator you can use to predict how the future is likely to unfold. Now in your mind, I need you to fast forward their personality and pre-figure how the future would unfold assuming you were in a love relationship. It is all-predictable; just unfold their core values, beliefs, interests, dreams, the way they think, and assume you were living together and take pictures of that scene. You do not need to be a psychic or an astrologer to do this; you can learn to look into your future. Fast forward your life with them a few more years and take more pictures. Fast forward into old age and take more pictures. Enlarge all those pictures of you two together.

1) What do you see?

2) Are you happy?

3) Are you living your dream?

And here, you are shaping the quality of your future and your family. Even though he or she may be a good person, if they do not match with the images in your vision, then it is smarter to cut your losses here than to force a mismatch. At this stage, it is smarter to go back into the open range and search for your true lover, who is still out there looking for you. As you do this over, make sure that you are in agreement with the profile of the person in your blueprint. Focus on checking and double checking their reputation if you have to and eliminate the possibility of taking on the unacceptable baggage you cannot accommodate in your future love. Also, make sure that you are truly understood on all your specific needs, expectations, and plans from a futuristic point of view.

This critical talk and evaluation step enables you to get full knowledge about your lover, and from my findings, knowing each other's true identity is one factor that creates inner peace and enables you to protect your heart and future from pain.

If at any time you find any red flags you cannot tolerate in your future, this is the best time to cut your losses. Remember, this Universe has billions of great single men and women looking for a smart lover like you; you do not have to compromise your future for whatever emotional reason. If you are happy, you can now move on to the next step.

CHAPTER 11
Step 7: The Timing Factor

From the time you meet to the time you decide to commit your love to her/him, you should allow some period to get to know more details about each other and to be sure that the person you are attempting to take home is the dreamed person you wanted and not an impostor who will change later. This period varies from person to person, depending on your needs, your maturity, your experience, the pre-marital knowledge you possess, and how fast you are in gathering all the basic information you need to be able to make your winning lifetime decision.

This period also enables you to know their character, because as you know, many men and women will not tell you about their biggest baggage for fear that you may not love them once you know. Moreover, this timing step is the last lifeline you have to unveil these hidden masks, to confirm their true character, to prove whether she/he can keep their word, and to confirm to you whether you can really trust the quality of your destiny in their hands. This time is the last lifeline that helps you to reduce the unpleasant surprises out of your future.

This is what you need to do in step # 7: You should keep asking a lot, especially about their current plans and dreams for the future. Your purpose here again is to confirm that you are both compatible, regarding your needs and expectations from your future together. Before you decide to commit your timeless love to them, keep doing this forward thinking exercise.

Sit quietly and keep on simulating their past behavior and character, and mentally picture how your relationship will unfold in the future. What do you see?

1) Are you pleased with the forecast pictures you are seeing?

2) Do you see true love and harmony unfolding in your relationship?

3) By the way, are their words consistent with their actions?

Can you really trust them with your precious heart and destiny? And if you have been asking for guidance in your decision, the Universe will answer your questions through so many avenues. All you have to do is to listen deeply for the answers. Just listen deeply.

Here again is the advantage of delaying physical intimacy! You are not yet emotionally attached to a deeper level, and quitting the relationship now is less costly than breaking up after wedlock. Just keep talking; this time will bring you all the answers you have been looking for and confirm to you the right decision to make.

This step helps you to discover their authenticity and dramatically lowers the risk of falling in love with an impostor, who is going to pretend to be the ideal prospect you were looking for, and then become a different person after your wedding day. Most importantly, this step enables you to confirm that you are both willing to trust your entire destiny in each other's hands, and it is not one person's desire for total commitment.

Now I believe you can see here that being patient and allowing this time to reassure you of your final decision is certainly smarter than rushing into marriage and then rushing to get out at a painful cost. If you are not happy now, do not leave it to chance; this is your best time to cut your losses and go back to the open range of singles. On the other hand, if you are pleased with her or him as a potential partner, your inner knower will tell you - you are right.

Just a thought: If you cannot figure anything out, it may be a good idea to consult an older friend or relative to help you see what you are not seeing. Sometimes, it is easier for another person to see the obvious things that we do not see about the person we have feelings for. Please, whatever they advise you, do not argue with them; just shut up and listen for the answers. If you are happy, you can now proceed to Step #8.

CHAPTER 12
Step 8. Engagement

The purpose of this Step is to show your commitment for each other and to express your well-thought out desire to take your relationship to the next higher level and be as emotionally attached and loving as you wish. In addition, it is to inform your family members and friends about your commitment to your smart choice and your readiness to invest your future in each other.

At this stage, you are confident that she or he is your true love and meets the profile of your desired husband or wife. Depending on your cultural practices and financial resources, make it an exciting ceremony, and celebrate this major step towards the success in your love relationship. Do what you have to do to make it fun and an event worth remembering. Then you can start planning your future together and make plans for total commitment and/or with a wedding.

The benefits of engagement are that it assures you both to be in agreement regarding your mutual desire to love each other forever.

Second, it also stretches your mind to start thinking bigger than before, bigger than you as one person do, and to start planning for your future as a partnership. Third, it informs the other single men and women that you are already committed to someone else, and this helps to reduce the pressures from those who are asking for dates. Now you can schedule a day to celebrate your total commitment in the next Step # 9.

CHAPTER 13
Step 9. Total Commitment

The purpose of this step is to confirm each other's love and commitment. Commitment to grow stronger and total commitment to build a family as one in the traditional family spirit.

There are many books on how to plan a wedding. Visit the library near you and read on the best options of making it happen, depending on your financial ability. Always remember, your ultimate goal is to be happy. Make it big, but make sure you do not spend much more money than you can afford to pay back within the agreed period. If you end up with too many bills you cannot afford to pay after the wedding, you are likely to end up stressed and seeing your spouse as the source of this big debt. Just remember that the cost of your wedding is not as important as the peace of mind after the ceremony. Keep the expenses within the limits you can afford; you will have more joy that way.

What are the benefits of this step #9? This step gives your wife or husband total confidence that you are truly his/hers forever and not just in mere words. It is a beautiful ceremony that reaffirms your decision to truly love each other forever; it is a true confirmation that you chose her/him as the best on this planet. You are saying to each other that you are now a team, and you are going to win together as a new family. It is a great achievement of great value and joys, dreamed by nearly everybody, but most have not been able to find their ideal woman or man to propose to.

At this stage, you have done the right thing. You should stay excited and feel good about your successful self for the rest of your life. However, your work has just started for both of you. You must remain committed and work on making it the best love relationship you dreamed of and work every day to make it victorious. So what happens afterwards?

CHAPTER 14
Step 10. Enjoying Your Love & Counting Your Blessings

This is the rest of your lifetime, and it is a period that requires both of you to develop a new thinking style that is specifically targeted at creating continuous growth and success on a daily basis.

This period requires you to mature in the mind to start thinking in terms of "we as a one entity" and forget your single person's mindset where you would not care about another person's feelings. This is also the only stage where you should work on compromising to make sure that you both win and that no one is a loser in your love relationship. You should work hard every day to ensure that you keep prospering each other's heart with warm thoughts and kind feelings for each other.

However, I found out that even after marrying your true husband or wife, many people still make poor decisions, because they do not know how to keep their lover successfully. I have found out that keeping a lover successfully is a skill anyone can learn. You have to know what you are doing every step of the way, every single day. Therefore, in an effort to support you on your journey to a brighter future for you and your family, I captured the thinking styles of the smart spouses, who had been happily married from 10 to 50 years. They had mastered how to strategically focus their thoughts to enable them to become a better spouse and prosper their marriage skillfully.

Since your dream is to create a great marriage, it was recommended that duplicating their successful strategies could also lead you to attract the same kind of marital lifestyle they are enjoying. Their success mindsets are documented in my next new book I intend to title *How to Build a Joyful Family*. I hope this book will help you use their proven insights and strategies to create more richness in your marriage. This book will teach you how to become a Smart Spouse and how to make your world better and brighter every day. It is a must-read for anyone who desires a Joyful Family.

As I conclude, I am now requesting you to make a promise to yourself that you will make a decision to activate your genius to find your true lover. No matter how long it takes, you are not going to sabotage yourself. You will date skillfully and be sure that your ideal choice will also find you ideal to them before you commit into wedlock. I am confident that this thinking style will help you to make your best decision. I believe that you will be very successful in creating a rich love relationship as your destiny, because it is all predictable. Sure, you can do it. Read this book often, use whatever techniques make sense to you, and take personal responsibility in shaping your destiny the way you want it, because you can.

Before you go, I need one favor from you. If you found this book useful, please help me and tell your special friends about Skillful Dating, because together, we can end this painful trend of one out of every two marriages failing, lots of domestic violence cases, and heartbroken people. You too can empower your friends to create a great love relationship, thus increasing the number of happier families and joyful communities. It has been a big pleasure to me spending this time with you, and I believe you have gained something from this book. My hope is that you will use this base knowledge to create a joyful future for you and your family.

Friend, I wish you the best love, all the days of your life.

With much love,

Alex K. Mugume

Alex is also available for teaching engagements and personal consultations. Feel free to participate in my blog and subscribe to the Skillful Dating Newsletter so you are the first to know about the free webinars (seating is always limited). NOTE: This book is also available as an audio book at Amazon.com, Audible.com. iTunes.com, bookstores, most public libraries and also at http://www.SkillfulDating.com

ABOUT THE AUTHOR

Alex Mugume believes that Skillful Dating is the answer to the challenges in today's dating world because it helps people minimize the odds of a mismatch. The wisdom in this book will help make this world a better place with more people finding their ideal romantic partners for happier and more lasting love relationships or marriages, and eventually make divorce and domestic violence plagues of the past.

Alex has never attended a class in psychology or philosophy. He stumbled upon this dating knowledge while sharing his best approach to matchmaking using a strategic, futuristic and risk management mindset. People were intrigued by the logic behind every step of the approach and how this made matchmaking so easy and predictable. They were impressed that they could now screen a potential lover without first becoming intimate! The interest in the approach led to this dating knowledge and in writing the book, *Skillful Dating for Smart Singles*.

Alex lives in Chicago with his family. He has a background in building and civil engineering, and his areas of specialty are high-level strategy and project risk management. He loves teaching and simplifying complex challenges to help manage and increase future project success.

Please help share this dating knowledge with your single friends. Help Alex by lobbying your leaders about teaching Skillful Dating in every High School.

More information and contact information for Alex Mugume is at http://www.SkillfulDating.com

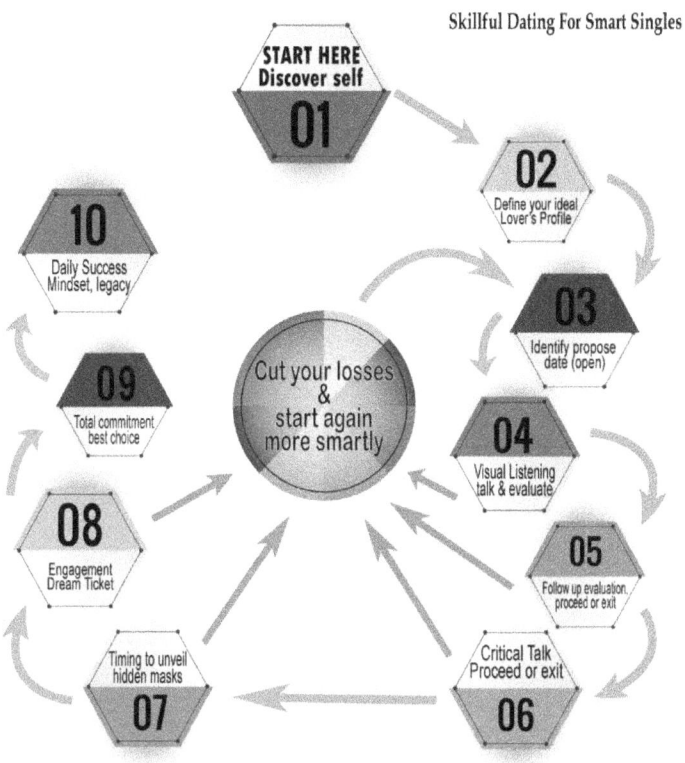

Figure 1.
The Skillful Dating Model (SDM)

© Alex Mugume

www.ingramcontent.com/pod-product-compliance
Lightning Source LLC
Chambersburg PA
CBHW051708040426
42446CB00008B/781